Float Like A Butterfly

Muhammad Ali: The Greatest Boxer In History

Tony Fitzsimmons

Table of Contents

The End And The Beginning

The Greatest

Vietnam

Return

A Change In Direction

Politics And Religion

Man And Icon

In His Own Words

The End And The Beginning

On June 10 2016, hundreds of people lined the streets of Louisville, Kentucky, as a procession of black cars drove slowly by. A hearse, strewn with flowers placed by onlookers, carried the mortal remains of Muhammad Ali, born Cassius Marcellus Clay, Jnr.

The procession wound its way to Cave Hill Cemetery, where the ex-boxer known to the world as 'The Greatest' was laid to rest in a private ceremony.

It was a fitting end to a life that, powerful as it was, had really shone outside of the limelight.

Before the procession Ali was commemorated by a Muslim funeral or *jenazah*.

Some 14000 people of different races and creeds gathered to hear the prayer for the dead recited at the funerals of all Muslims:

'O God, forgive our living and our dead, those who are present among us and those who are absent, our young and our old, our males and our females. O God, whoever You keep alive, keep him alive in Islam, and whoever You cause to die, cause him to die with faith. O God, do not deprive us of the reward and do not cause us to go astray after this. O God, forgive him and have mercy on him, keep him safe and sound and forgive him, honor his rest and ease his entrance; wash him with water and snow and hail, and cleanse him of sin as a white garment is cleansed of dirt. O God, give him a home better than his home and a family better than his family. O God, admit him to Paradise and protect him from the torment of the grave and the torment of Hell-fire; make his grave spacious and fill it with light.'

Sherman Jackson, a Muslim scholar from the University of Southern California said of Ali's passing 'Something solid, something big, beautiful and life-affirming has left this world.'

In a live Facebook broadcast President Barack Obama said 'It's very rare where a figure captures the imagination of the entire world.'

Other men and women of status lined up to pay their respects, including former

President Bill Clinton, comedian Billy Crystal and President of Turkey, Tayyip Erdogan.

Also present was civil rights activist and Senator Jesse Jackson, wrote of him six days earlier 'The world has lost one of the greatest heroes of all time. He sacrificed, the nation benefited. He was a champion in the ring, but, more than that, a hero beyond the ring. When champions win, people carry them off the field on their shoulders. When heroes win, people ride on their shoulders. We ride on Muhammad Ali's shoulders.'

So who was this man who was known as the 'people's champion'? What was it about him that earned the respect, if not the love, of America and the world.

He did not always have that respect. He never sought it, in fact.

At times he was divisive. He was brash and cocky. He was confrontational. He was a showman, certainly, but also man of intense conviction.

He was born Cassius Marcellus Clay Jnr. on January 17 1942. He took his somewhat unusual name from his father, who in turn was named after a politician who lived from 1810 – 1903.

This Clay served in the Kentucky House of Representatives for a time and also as a US ambassador to Russia.

A staunch abolitionist, Clay refused to accept an appointment as Major-general during the US Civil War unless President Lincoln agreed to free all the slaves in the southern states. Clay accepted his posting and Lincoln did issue the Emancipation Proclamation in 1862.

Later in life Clay spoke out against the corrupting power of industrialists and the military intervention of the United States in Haiti.

He had a reputation as a rebel and an activist.

Though his devotion to emancipation may have inspired Muhammad Ali's ancestors, Cassius Clay did not entirely impress him.

When changing his own name, he said of Senator Clay that he 'held on to white supremacy…. Why should I keep my white slave master's name visible and my black ancestors invisible, unknown, unhonoured?'

One could also have pointed out that Senator Clay also owned slaves for a time.

Cassius Clay Snr. (1912 – 1990) was a Louisville painter and musician. He drank and played hard, leading often to brushes with the law.

His wife and Muhammad's mother, Odessa Lee Grady (1917 – 1994), married Cassius after working as a domestic.

Odessa was a Christian, and her influence on her children was strong. 'My mother is a Baptist,' Muhammad Ali said, 'and when I was growing up, she taught me all she knew about God. Every Sunday, she dressed me up, took me and my brother to church, and taught us the way she thought was right. She taught us to love people and treat everybody with kindness. She taught us it was wrong to be prejudiced or hate. I've changed my religion and some of my beliefs since then, but her God is still God; I just call him by a different name. And my mother, I'll tell you what I've told people for a long time. She's a sweet, fat, wonderful woman, who loves to cook, eat, make clothes, and be with family. She doesn't drink, smoke, meddle in other people's business, or bother anyone, and there's no one who's been better to me my whole life.'

Muhammad had one sibling, a brother, Rudolph Arnet. Rudolph was a year younger than Cassius. Like his elder brother, he became a boxer. And like his brother, he changed his birth name, becoming Rahman Ali.

Racial segregation was observed in Kentucky in the period when Cassius was growing up. Indeed it was the norm in both the US North and South. His mother related a story of him as a child being refused a drink of water because he was black. She said this had a profound effect on him.

Another event had a profound effect on him.

In August 1955 a fourteen-year-old African American boy, Emmet Till, was tortured and drowned in the town of Money, Mississippi.

In the subsequent trial for murder, the accused, Bryant and Millam, were acquitted by an all-white and all-male jury. One juror remarked, 'if we hadn't stopped to drink pop, it wouldn't have taken that long.

Bryant and Millam later confessed to the murder, when it was clear that they could not be tried again.

The murder did much to intensify pressure on the US Government to address the issue of racial discrimination.

Cassius's boxing career began with an encounter with Joe E. Martin, a boxing coach and Louisville police officer.

In 1954, Clay, 12 years old, rode to the Louisville Service Club Convention on his bike, with a friend. While he was there he discovered that his bicycle had been stolen. Hot with anger, he told Martin, who was in a boxing gym in the basement.

He told Martin that he would track the thief done and give him a good thumping.

'Well, do you know how to fight?' Martin asked. No, the boy replied. No doubt recognizing a frustrated youth in need of direction Martin asked 'Why don't you learn something about fighting before you and make any hasty challenges?'

At first Clay ignored the invitation. But after seeing some amateur boxers on television he changed his mind. His imagination was fired by dreams of glory, and he asked Martin to train him.

Joe Elsby Martin (1916 – 1996) had been the boxing coach at Columbia Gym since 1938. He coached many troubled youths as a mean of giving them discipline and focus. He took

Cassius under his wing, coaching him for six years.

Martin's wife Christine recalled her memories of Clay many years later.

'Cassius was a very-easy-to-get-along-with fellow. Very easy to handle. Very polite. Whatever you asked him to do, that's what he'd do.'

She related that he was a deeply reflective boy. 'On trips most of the boys were out looking around, seeing what they could get into, whistling at pretty girls. But Cassius didn't believe in that. He carried his Bible everywhere he went, and while the other boys were out looking around, he was sitting and reading his Bible.'

Clay's first fight, after only six weeks of training, was against one Ronnie O'Keefe, The bout lasted three rounds.

He won, but by a split decision.

An exhilarated Clay announced to the onlookers, and to the world, that he'd be 'the greatest of all time.'

The Greatest

Clay's career took off at a meteoric rate. By 1960 he had the amateur boxing title, the Golden Gloves, in Kentucky six times. He won the national Golden Gloves title twice.

Further, he won a National Athletic Union title.

In his amateur career he had 100 wins and only five losses.

The height of his amateur glory was achieved in the 1960 Rome Olympics.

At the age of only 18 won gold in the light heavyweight event, beating Zbigniew Pietrzykowski of Poland.

In Rome Clay had his first look at the wider world and observed that racial discrimination was not only an issue in the United States but elsewhere.

South Africa, for example, would not field black athletes because of its apartheid policy.

But Clay would have seen signs of an awakening as well.

The African American Wilma Rudolph became the first American to win three gold medals in track and field. Rafer Johnson carried the Olympic Torch into the stadium.

This was to be the last Olympics in which South Africa would compete. It was banned by the International Olympic Committee from the 196 and all subsequent Games, until 1992 when apartheid ended.

Clay must have wondered why his own country could not be so aggressive against its own apartheid.

Cassius Clay himself did much to focus attention on racial issues and the status of African Americans. America could not help but watch him and pay attention to him.

Commentators observed that he moved in the ring 'with lightning speed, firing left and rights in stunning combinations'. This would later become enshrined in boxing folklore as the 'Ali shuffle.'

Clay had been lionized in Europe. But when he returned to the United States he was again a second class citizen, and he felt it.

In a 1975 autobiography Ali stated that he had been refused service in a White-only restaurant shortly after his return. He threw his gold medal in the Ohio River. It would be replaced for him in 1996.

In 1960 the Civil Rights movement was gaining momentum.

In October iconic activist Dr. Martin Luther King was arrested with 50 others during a sit-in in Rich Department Store, Atlanta. He was later freed by US Attorney-General Robert F. Kennedy.

In July of 1960 Elijah Muhammad (1897 – 1975), the son of Georgian sharecroppers and leader of the Nation of Islam, called for an all-black state.

For the nation of Islam, which in 1960 may have had 100,000 members and now has about 50,000, the Islamic religion is a vehicle for African Americans to understand and empower themselves.

The Nation of Islam was founded in 1930 by one Wallace Fard Muhammad. He founded NOI to 'teach the downtrodden and defenseless Black people a thorough knowledge of God and of themselves, and to put them on the road to Self-Independence with a superior culture and higher civilization than they had previously experienced.'

The Nation takes the basic tenants of Islam and joins them with some peculiar to itself. It believes the founder is the Mahdi, the prophet who will precede the day of judgement.

It also inverts White supremacism by holding that the original race of humans was

Black. The white races are an aberration from the divine plan.

Clay first heard of the Nation of Islam in 1959 and attended his first meeting in 1961.

In 1962 Clay first met Malcolm X. Malcolm X, born Malcolm Little in 1925, was one of the leaders of NOI at the time.

After converting to Islam and completing a pilgrimage to Mecca. Malcolm X called himself el- hajj Malik-el-Shabazz.

Like Clay, the young Malcolm X burned with passion against the white establishment. His family fled from the Klu-Klux Klan, and his father may have been murdered by White supremacists. He certainly thought so.

He wanted to be a lawyer, but he dropped out of high school after his teacher told him that law was 'no realistic goal for a nigger.'

He drifted into crime: drugs, racketeering, robbery and pimping.

Eventually he was arrested and imprisoned.

In prison he learned about the Nation of Islam through his family. He wrote to Elijah Muhammad, who encouraged him to embrace Islam. He became a member of the Nation of Islam.

His activism began even before he was released from prison. He wrote to President Truman decrying the Korean War, prompting the FBI to create a file on him.

From 1950 he began to sign himself Malcolm 'X.' He explained that the letter stood or his unknown ancestral name, refusing to use the surname that had been given to him by the White establishment.

After his release in 1952 Malcolm X became a powerful activist within the Nation of Islam. An eloquent speaker and physically impressive, he recruited many into the NOI. The phenomenal rise in membership in the 50s and 60s was due in no small part to him.

His voice on racial issues was being heard throughout the United States and beyond. The representatives of several nations spoke with him, including President Gamal Abdel Nasser of Egypt, Ahmed Sekou Toure, President of Guinea, and Kenneth Kaunda, who would become the first President of Zambia.

Malcolm X met publicly with the Communist Fidel Castro and accepted an invitation to visit Cuba. This infuriated the White House.

In his activity Malcolm X did not just advocate equality under the law, as the Martin Luther King movement did, but complete liberation from White domination.

This appealed to Clay, and Malcolm X became his mentor.

Soon Nation of Islam members, including Malcolm X, were seen in Clay's entourage. However, he was refused membership on account of his boxing.

That changed when Clay took the heavyweight championship from Sonny Liston (†1970) in 1964.

Liston was considered one of the greatest heavyweights of all time and an overpowering presence in the ring.

Clay, despite his amateur record and the 1960 Olympics was stilled considered a newcomer and an untested athlete. He had been bested by Sonny Banks (the first boxer to do so) and had been knocked down by Henry Cooper.

The sports reporters disliked Clay and predicted that he would lose. One journalist said the match would only last one round.

Clay's quick, light boxing style – 'float like a butterfly, sting like a bee' – was deemed inadequate to beat Liston.

The night before the fight, Harvey Jones, the sparring partner of the young man already known as the 'Louisville Lip', presented a poem by Clay.

Clay comes out to meet Liston and Liston starts to retreat,

If Liston goes back an inch farther he'll end up in a ringside seat.

Clay swings with a left,

Clay swings with a right,

Just look at young Cassius carry the fight.

Liston keeps backing but there's not enough room,

It's a matter of time until Clay lowers the boom.

Then Clay lands with a right, what a beautiful swing,

And the punch raised the bear clear out of the ring.

Liston still rising and the ref wears a frown,

But he can't start counting until Sonny comes down.

Now Liston disappears from view, the crowd is getting frantic

But our radar stations have picked him up somewhere over the Atlantic.

Who on Earth thought, when they came to the fight,

That they would witness the launching of a human satellite.

Hence the crowd did not dream, when they laid down their money,

That they would see a total eclipse of Sonny.

A few weeks before the fight Clay's association with the Nation of Islam (then also known as the Black Muslims) became known. Clay's father was reported as saying 'they (NOI) ruined my two boys… Muslims tell my boys to hate white people; to hate women..'

Clay's affiliation disturbed the fight's promoters, and they threatened to cancel the fight if he did not publicly distance himself from NOI.

He would not agree to do this. However, he did agree to make no explicit statements about the Nation of Islam, and Malcolm X kept a low profile until the fight was done.

The fight occurred on February 25, 1964 at the Convention Hall, Miami, Florida. Clay weighed in at 210 lb (95 kg). Liston was 218 lb (99kg).

The match ended in the seventh round when Liston, bested by Clay's light shuffling, quick-jabbing technique, failed to answer the bell. Clay was declared the winner by a technical knock-out.

It was the first time since 1919 that a heavyweight had been defeated without leaving the stool.

'Eat your words!' victorious Clay told reporters. 'I'm the greatest! I shook up the world!'

Two days after the fight Clay announced that he had joined the Nation of Islam. His membership had been approved the day before.

Why did the fight change the decision to accept Clay? Perhaps Elijah Muhammad and the rest of the NOI leadership felt that Clay's victory gave them a powerful platform from which to speak.

Elijah Muhammad announced that Cassius Clay had renounced his name and taken another. From now on he would be known as Muhammad Ali.

Mohammad means 'worthy of all praise'. Ali means 'the greatest.'

To journalists who refused to use his new name he declared 'I am America. I am the part you won't recognize. But get used to me. Black, confident, cocky; my name, not yours; my religion, not yours; my goals, my own; get used to me.'

Vietnam

In 1964 Malcolm X had been having doubts about the Nation of Islam and about Elijah Muhammad in particular.

The year previously he had learned that Muhammad was in relationships with at least six women in the NOI. He had children from some of them.

X was disillusioned. He had regarded Muhammad as a living prophet. He had lead many into the organization because of him, and now he discovered that he was a fraud.

On November 22 1963 President John F. Kennedy was assassinated. Malcolm X outraged a mourning nation by declaring of Kennedy that he 'never foresaw that the chickens would come to roost so soon.'

Elijah Muhammad stepped in, forbidding X to speak publicly. Ostensibly this was to protect the organization, though Malcolm X believed it was an opportunistic attempt to silence him about Elijah Muhammad's liaisons.

At this time X was mentoring Ali prior to the fight with Liston.

Shortly after the fight, in March 1964, X announced that he had terminated his membership in the Nation of Islam.

X and Ali had cultivated a strong friendship, and X believed Ali would leave NOI as well.

He was wrong. With all the ardor of a fresh convert he stood by Muhammad and his organization. He believed X was being disloyal.

Later in the year, X went on pilgrimage to Mecca. There he re-discovered Islam, a religion that embraced people of all races. He met 'blonde-haired, blue-eyed men that I could call brothers.'

In that same year Ali and X met for the last time, in Acra, Ghana.

Seeing Ali, X exclaimed 'Brother Muhammad! Brother Muhammad!'

Hard-faced, Ali replied 'Brother Malcolm, you shouldn't have crossed the Honorable Elijah Muhammad.' And he walked away in the company of Elijah Muhammad's son.

X returned to the United States with a new vision of Black liberation, a vision that included all races.

On February 21 1965 Malcolm X was assassinated. Speaking in the Audubon Ballroom in Manhattan, he was shot 59 times at close range by three gunmen.

All three assassins were members of the Nation of Islam. To this day it is not known who, if anyone, ordered the killing. Malcolm X's family has always maintained that Louis Farrakhan (b.1933), a notable NOI leader, had a hand in the affair, and some of Farrakhan's statements seem to suggest that he did.

Muhammad Ali was to say that breaking his friendship with Malcolm X was the biggest regret of his life.

'I wish I'd been able to tell Malcolm I was sorry,' he said in a 2004 interview. 'He was right about so many things. But he was killed before I got the chance.'

At another time Ali said that Malcolm X was a 'visionary, ahead of us all.'

And again he has said 'Malcolm was the first to discover the truth, that color doesn't make a man a devil. It is the heart, soul and mind that define a person'.

In 1975 Elijah Muhammad died and his son Warith Deen Muhammad bean to steer the Nation of Islam toward the path walked by Malcolm X.

The members of the NOI embraced Sunni Islam under his leadership. Sunni Islam preaches the brotherhood and sisterhood of all Muslims regardless of race.

Ali would come to embrace this belief too, but for now he continued to espouse the superiority of the Black race.

In 1974 he was interviewed on *Parkinson*. In the course of the interview he told Michael Parkinson that he had no white friends. He had white 'associates'. The white man in America was the 'blonde-haired, blue-eyed Devil.'

His boxing career too courted controversy.

He successfully defended his title against Floyd Patterson (1935-2006) on November 22 1965 but was criticized afterward for appearing to toy with his opponent.

The World Boxing Association heavyweight champion Ernie Terell (1939 – 2014) agreed to fight Ali. The bout was scheduled for March 29 1966.

In February the Louisville Draft Board reclassified Ali so that he was now eligible to be drafted for service in Vietnam. Previously his reading and writing skills were deemed sub-standard, thus precluding him from service.

Ali used the occasion to express his opposition to the draft and his opinions on the war in Vietnam.

The United States began sending regular combat units to South Vietnam in 1965, though it had maintained a military presence there since the 1950s.

'War is against the teaching of the Qur'an,' Ali declared. 'I ain't got nothing against no

Viet Cong. No Viet Cong never called me nigger.'

Public outrage was strong and the media was tiring of this self-aggrandizing braggart. The focus was not on the morality of the war, but on him.

The Illinois Athletic Commission canceled the fight with Terell, citing technical reasons.

Undaunted, Ali went on a tour of Canada and Europe, winning a series of championship bouts.

One of the challengers was Henry Cooper in Britain.

After felling Ali with a left hook, Cooper fended off a series of blows that injured his left eye.

With his opponent covered in blood, Ali continued to jab at the injured eye. It was to be a foretaste of the merciless attack on Terrell in 1967.

When he returned to the United States he fought Cleveland Williams in Houston on November 14 1966.

Williams hadn't fought for a year and was recovering from an injury. He had been shot by a police officer in a scuffle and had lost ten feet of small intestine as well as sustained permanent kidney damage.

The fight lasted three rounds.

Ali and Terrell did finally fight, again in Houston. Terrell had not been defeated in five years and had successfully seen off many of Ali's opponents.

In the lead up to the bout Terrell called his challenger 'Clay.' This was an innocent mistake. Ali and Terrell had been friends, roommates and sparring partners. Terrell had not known Ali except as 'Cassius Clay'.

But this stung Ali, who said that he wanted to 'torture' Terrell. 'A clean knockout is too good for him,' he said.

Throughout the fight Ali kept taunting Terrell. 'What's my name, Uncle Tom? What's my name?' Uncle Tom was the title character in an 1852 novel by Harriet Beecher Stowe. He was a slave, and the name has become an insult to signify a subservient person (Terrell was Afro-American).

Commentators described the match as 'one of the ugliest boxing fights'. It seemed like

Ali was indeed trying to inflict the greatest amount of pain he could.

Ali had thumbed Terrell in the eye so that he had to fight half-blind. He also rubbed his eyes into the ropes and spat on his bloody boots.

'I could see two or three of him because of the damage,' said Terrell years later. 'And trust me, one is enough.'

Spectators saw the undisciplined fury of the teenage boy whose bicycle had been stolen 12 years ago.

Sports journalist Tex Maule would later write 'it was a wonderful demonstration of boxing skill and a barbarous display of cruelty.'

Next Ali fought Zora Folley. Folley was a gentleman boxer, uncommon at the time. He was a decorated hero of the Korean War and led a clean life.

A repetition of the Terrell fight against this honorable man would destroy what was left of Ali's already sullied reputation. After knocking Folley out in the seventh round Ali had the grace to remark, through his coach, that he was 'one heckuva fighter.' He also expressed relief that he had not fought Folley 10 years earlier.

In 1967 Ali was ordered to report for induction in the US Army. He did appear at Houston for induction on April 28. However, he refused to answer his name when called.

After being warned that refusal to answer would mean five years imprisonment and a fine of $10 000 (almost $72 000 in 2017) he continued to refuse another two times.

He was arrested on the spot. On the same day the New York State Athletic Commission suspended his boxing license for three years. Furthermore, his heavyweight title was taken away.

Other boxing organizations quickly followed.

On June 20 1967 Ali was tried. The jury found him guilty only after 21 minutes of deliberation.

A Court of Appeals upheld the conviction.

Then Ali appealed to the Supreme Court. On June 28 1971 it ruled on the case, the title of which seemed to sum up Muhammad Ali: *Clay vs. United States.*

The Court ruled against the Government on the grounds that it had not given any reason for not recognizing Ali's claim to be a conscientious objector.

In its ruling the Court declared that 'moral and ethical objection to war was as valid as religious objection.'

The decision was unanimous.

Politically and socially the decision was dynamite. Opposition to the war in Vietnam was mounting, though support for it was still strong, and conscientious objectors were empowered.

Ali's resistance to the draft contributed powerfully to the energy of the Civil Rights Movement.

Ali now found himself a leader of that movement.

Previously Ali had not been active beyond his involvement in the Nation of Islam.

That began to change after 1968.

Martin Luther was assassinated on April 4 1968. Outrage followed, manifested in rioting.

Attempting to head off further unrest the Government paid homage to King (though the FBI had attempted to undermine and discredit him).

President Lyndon B Johnson hurriedly signed the Civil Rights Act into law on April 11 1968. It had only been passed by Congress the day before.

King and Ali were not willing allies. Doctor King denounced the Nation of Islam for encouraging African Americans to abandon Christianity. He criticized it for its refusal to include Whites in any resolution of civil rights issues.

He declared that 'the hatred and despair of the black nationalist' was inimical to the cause, which should be based on love.

King's efforts toward equality with whites in one country were derided by Ali. 'I'm not going to get killed trying to force myself on people who don't want me,' he said. 'Integration is wrong. White people don't want it, the Muslims don't want it. So what's wrong with the Muslims?'

Nevertheless, King and Ali shared much in common. They both received death threats.

They were both under surveillance from the FBI, and they both opposed the war.

Both believed the intervention in Vietnam to be an imperialist war initiated by and for the benefit of white people.

Despite their differences the two came together on the war issue.

Ali's stance on the draft baptized him into activism. He felt he could no longer be silent. He and King met at a rally in Louisville, Kentucky, Ali's hometown.

'In your struggle for freedom, justice and equality, I am with you,' said Ali. 'I came to Louisville because I could not remain silent while my own people, many I grew up with, many I went to school with, many my blood relatives, were being beaten, stomped and kicked in the streets simply because they want freedom, and justice and equality in housing.'

With King dead, Ali was now one of the focal points of the Civil Rights Movement.

In the late sixties and early seventies Ali's attitude toward whites as the 'blue-eyed devil' did not change. He remained devoted to Elijah Muhammad and the tenets of the separatist Nation of Islam.

A number of his beliefs did not fit well within the Civil Rights Movement, and seem odd, even outrageous to us today. For example, he held that interracial marriage was unnatural.

Indeed, one might make the argument that had Muhammad Ali been in the ring in the present day he would never have risen to iconic status. Instead he would have been labeled a racist and a hater.

Back then however the concept of Black Supremacism turned America on its head, and perhaps provided a mirror by which White America could see itself.

In any case Ali he could still authentically speak out on civil rights issues and against what he saw as a white imperialist war.

Return

While under suspension Ali did engage in a boxing match, though not an officially recognized one.

This match was a meticulously staged event, the result of negotiations with a boxing promoter and radio producer, Murray Woroner. Woroner wanted to film a fight between Rocky Marciano, who held the world heavyweight title from 1952 – 1956.

Ali and Marciano were the only undefeated heavyweights at the time.

Since it was technically a fictional fight it did not violate the ban on Ali fighting.

Ali and Marciano were filmed acting out every possible scenario during the match and a computer calculated the probability of the final outcome.

The final result was broadcast on closed-circuit television on January 20 1970. In the United States and Canada viewers saw a version where Marciano knocked out Ali. In Europe they saw Ali knock out Marciano.

It is difficult to imagine Ali relishing the project, particularly as someone who prided himself on being 'the greatest' being bested by a white man before a US audience.

Indeed, he was angered by the result. He claimed American viewers were equally angered by Marciano being portrayed as the winner.

He began defamation proceedings against Woroner. This was ironic as the whole project had arisen from a defamation suit.

Ali had sued Woroner for $1000 000. In a fictional radio program Woroner had Ali defeated in the ring. Ali settled out of court in return for $10 000 and collaboration in the staged fight.

Ali dropped defamation proceedings after the fight when the filmmakers decided to destroy all remaining prints.

Muhammad Ali continued to regret his participation in what must have been the strangest fight of his career.

But if Ali's glory was tarnished by the episode, it certainly recovered after his famous fight with Joe Frazier.

Billed as 'The Fight of the Century', Ali's first encounter with Frazier took place on March 8 1971.

His past suspension, if not forgiven by the public, was now at least forgotten for the sake of seeing a spectacle.

Typically, Ali denigrated his opponent before the fight, calling Frazier a 'dumb tool of the white establishment,' and 'too dumb to be a champ.' He also called him 'Uncle Tom,' a label he gave to many of his perceived opponents, in and out of the ring.

Joe Frazier (1944 – 2011) had in fact perhaps a more profound experience of white oppression than Ali had.

Frazier was the son of sharecroppers. Ali was middle-class.

The land Frazier worked with his parents was, in his own words, 'white dirt...not worth a damn.' He had witnessed a 12-year-old black boy being whipped with a belt by a white man for accidentally damaging a tractor.

Frazier had begun his amateur career alone and without a penny, around the time that a young Clay was angry over the loss of his shiny new bicycle.

It was certainly hypocritical for Ali to be calling Frazier a tool of the establishment after he had made a bizarre deal with the white filming industry to fight a white heavyweight for the entertainment of a predominantly white audience.

Indeed, Frazier might have made the observation that Ali's whole career had been engineered in large part by the white establishment, and that he got his breakthrough his relationship with Joe Martin, a white coach.

But Frazier gave back as good as he got. He would later state that Ali's barbs were 'a cynical attempt to make me feel isolated from my own people.'

Ali dared to state 'I'm fighting for the little man in the ghetto,' to which Frazier responded, 'What the f____ does he know about the ghetto?'

Ali and Frazier's relationship remained acrimonious throughout their lives.

Both Frazier and Ali were undefeated in the ring.

Ali took a lot of pressure in the ring, more than any other time previously. Frazier was taking Ali's jabs.

In the eleventh round it seemed that a right hook had finished Ali, but Frazier hesitated to go in for the kill. Ali returned, but was struck by Frazier in the final round.

That punch, was, in the estimation of the referee, the hardest a man could take. But Ali was back on his feet in just three seconds.

His jaw swollen, he continued to take blow after blow until the fight was ended and Frazier declared the winner.

It was Ali's first professional defeat.

Ali refused to accept defeat, and in typical fashion, blamed the white establishment. It was a 'white man's decision,' he declared.

There had been more at stake than his career. Ali had portrayed Frazier as a front man, a puppet, for the establishment that did not understand the Civil Rights Movement and opposition to the Vietnam War.

Ali on the other hand was the champion of black, anti-war America.

The delineation was nowhere near as clear as Ali portrayed it, but it played to a political and social narrative, and many Americans saw Ali fighting for themselves.

But the defeat did him no harm at all. His supporters continued to see him as their hero. His detractors had the satisfaction of seeing him defeated, and so felt able to pay him some respect.

Possibly Ali would never have been able to face Frazier without the support of his wife of that time.

He and Belinda Boyd married in 1967. Boyd was 17. She came from Chicago and had a strict Muslim upbringing. She was at one time part of Elijah Muhammad's security team.

Ali had observed Boyd a few times but they never dated.

The marriage was arranged. 'He (Ali) just told me you are going to be my wife.'

'All I cared about was my horses,' she said, expressing her enthusiasm, or lack of it, for the match.

But she later grew to love him.

They had four children: Maryum, 7; twins Jamilla and Rasheda,5, and Ibn Muhammad, 3.

Boyd changed her name to Khalilah Comancho Ali.

In the year of their marriage Ali was stripped of his title.

This was not Ali's first marriage. On August 14 1964 he married Sonji Roi, a cocktail waitress, after only one date.

The marriage did not last long however. She challenged Ali on the teachings of Elijah Muhammad and the behavior Ali expected of a Muslim's wife.

'She wouldn't do what she was supposed to do,' Ali said. 'She wore lipstick; she went into bars; she dressed in clothes that were revealing and didn't look right'.

After their divorce in January 1966 Ali wrote to her 'You traded heaven for hell, baby.'

Khalihah might have had a more Muslim attitude toward what Ali expected of a woman, but it did nothing to stop Ali's roving eye.

She described the marriage and the subsequent divorce as 'rough'. She claimed Ali had children out of wedlock.

In 1974 Ali, then 32, began a relationship with 16-year-old Wanda Bolton (Aaisha). Claiming the Muslim right to have more than one wife, he married her and fathered a child, Khalihah.

In public she was supportive, and in the days of Ali's suspension and during the preparation for the fight against Frazier, she stood by him.

However, by the time Ali 'married' Aaisha Khalihah had had enough.

In 1975 Ali infuriated her by introducing his mistress Veronica Porche to the President of the Philippines Ferdinand Marcos as his wife.

Ali and Khalihah divorced in 1977. Ali then married Porche.

On January 28 1974 Ali challenged Joe Frazier again for the title.

Neither Ali nor Frazier seemed to have tempered their attitude toward each other.

The two were in the ABC studio for *Wide World of Sports* to review their first fight with commentator Howard Cosell.

Ali once again claimed that he had won the fight and said that the decision to award the victory to Frazier was racially motivated – a something strange claim considering that his opponent was also black.

During the show Ali called Joe ignorant. Clearly stung, Joe stood to confront him but did not lay a hand on Ali.

Ali tried to force Frazier back in his chair and the two wrestled to the ground. Both men were fined $5000 by the New York State Athletic Commission for 'deplorable conduct demeaning to boxing.'

In the fight itself at Madison Square Garden Ali used different tactics to those in the 1971 fight, bobbing and weaving to avoid the vicious left hook that had floored him at the last meeting.

The fight, though considered a fine spectacle, was nowhere near as dramatic as the first match. Ali had learned his lessons and beat Frazier by a unanimous decision of the judges.

Ali and Frazier would meet again in the year one more time, this time in Manila, Philippines, in 1975.

But for now Ali had his eyes set on George Foreman (b.1949).

Foreman had taken the heavyweight title from Frazier.

The 'Rumble in the Jungle', as the fight was billed, took place October 30 1974 in Kinshasa in the Republic of Zaire (now the Democratic Republic of Congo).Both fighters spent much time in Zaire training.

In particular they had to acclimatize to the tropical climate. In October Kinshasa temperatures can soar as high as 37% C (99 F).

The fight was promoted by Don King and was his first big promotion.

King, easily identified by his black suit, bow tie, gravity-defying hair and cigar, started his career in sports as an illegal bookmaker.

In 1954 King shot one of his gambling house employees in the back while the man was robbing him. A court declared the act 'justifiable homicide.'

Thirteen years later he was convicted of second-degree murder after stomping an employee to death. The employee owed him $600.

King's association with boxing began when he convinced Ali to engage in a charity fight for a hospital.

King secured the fight for Zaire and guaranteed the fighters $5000 000 each.

Ali was popular in Zaire, though the expectation was that Foreman would win.

Foreman's greatest strength was his sheer power. To counter this Ali avoided close range fighting. He opened with a series of right-hand leads.

Foreman found himself using his energy in punches that were mostly blocked by Ali.

In the eighth round Ali knocked Foreman's head up. Then he delivered a blow squarely to the face.

Foreman staggered and fell. He failed to make the count. Ali had won and recovered his title.

Once again, he was the greatest. And he let the world know.

A Change In Direction

On February 25 1975, Elijah Muhammad, leader of the Nation of Islam, died.

He was succeeded by his son, Warith Deen Muhammad (1933 – 2008), who almost immediately set about dismantling his father's organization.

The Nation of Islam may have empowered many African Americans and given them a sense of identity but it was also having a divisive and many would have said destructive influence.

Its Black Supremacist, anti-integration attitudes put it at odds not only with the Civil Rights Movement but with the wider Islamic world.

The principles of the Nation of Islam were bizarrely compatible with those of white supremacists. Elijah Muhammad allegedly met with the Klu Klux Klan to purchase land for NOI.

George Lincoln Rockwell (1918 – 1967), founder of the American Nazi Party, called Muhammad 'the Hitler of the Black Man.'

Elijah Muhammad taught that the original race of humans was black. One of these first inhabitants was called Yakub. Yakub, 'the devil', created white man after 600 years work in a laboratory.

Yakub was eventually expelled from paradise with his creations. These creatures, quite literally termed 'devils' by the Nation of Islam, went on to subjugate the earth.

Elijah Muhammad claimed that there was a platform above the earth, operated by 'men who never smile.' There were bombs on this platform, which would be dropped on the earth to end the reign of the devils.

Ali claimed to have seen this platform, 'a bright light darting in the sky'.

Warith Deen Muhammad rejected his father's separatist ideals. He changed the name of the organization several times, settling finally on the American Society of Muslims. This is the name by which it is known today.

His reforms were not universally accepted. Louis Farrakhan notably split from the group to continue the organization as Elijah Muhammad envisaged it. Farrakhan continues as leader to this day and still teaches that a separate black state, not integration, is the way forward.

One might imagine that a fiery spirit like Ali's would not have taken readily to a change in direction so sudden and so at odds with the faith that Ali had professed only 9 years earlier.

But Ali was willingly to consider Warith Deen's arguments, even though Elijah Muhammad had been his mentor. In 1991 he would state that Warith ' learned from his studies that his father wasn't teaching true Islam, and Wallace taught us the true meaning of the Quran. He showed that color don't matter. He taught that we're responsible for our own lives and it's no good to blame our problems on other people. And that sounded right to me so I followed

Wallace, but not everyone in the Nation felt that way. Some of the ministers didn't like what he was teaching. Jeremiah Shabazz didn't like it. Louis Farrakhan didn't like it either. They believed Elijah was a prophet, and they've kept the exact ways Elijah taught them. But I've changed what I believe, and what I believe in now is true Islam.'

One wonders whether Ali had already been thinking about these issues, and whether the idea of owning our problems struck a chord with him.

What is known is that Ali went on Hajj or pilgrimage to Mecca in 1972. There he encountered, as Malcolm X did, a huge number of Muslims of different ethnicities.

Hajj is mandatory on those Muslims who can afford to do it and who can support their families while away from their homes.

The word hajj means 'to intend a journey', both in a physical and spiritual sense.

It is the largest annual gathering of human beings in the world and is a powerful manifestation of worldwide Islamic solidarity.

When they arrive at Mecca all Muslims enter a state of holiness called *ihram.* All men don white seamless cloths and all perform the same rituals. This is to demonstrate the equality of all Muslims before God.

These rituals must have made a profound influence on Ali, as they did upon Malcolm X. Muslims from all continents gathering in solidarity to profess their faith and the fraternity of all Muslims.

On the subject of Ali's religion, we might wonder what influence it had on his boxing. His boxing rhetoric and style was so obviously aggressive that we might ask how Ali could reconcile his aggression with a religion that professed peace.

Indeed, boxing is frowned upon by not a few Islamic scholars.

We might remember that Elijah Muhammad was at first reluctant to accept Ali into the Nation of Islam on account of his boxing career.

We could also question why Ali would not go to Vietnam to fight people who he said had done him no harm yet he seemed eager to harm individuals, both whites and men of color, in the ring.

It has been speculated that Malcolm X persuaded Ali that his boxing career was something of a divine mission.

Before his fight with Sonny Liston in 1964 Ali proclaimed 'It is prophesized that I should win! I cannot be beaten!'

The use of the word 'prophesized' would seem to suggest more than pre-fight bravado and theatrics.

In their book *Muhammad Ali: The Glory Years* writers Felix Dennis and Don Atyeo suggest 'Malcolm X firmly implanted in Ali's mind the belief that he was invincible which must have been of enormous psychological advantage to a young fighter facing the awesome Sonny Liston. Ali became a fanatic and fanaticism greatly increased his resolve. By the time he learned that he was not invincible, Ali had matured enough to take the lesson in his stride. Conversely, the thought of having to face a dreaded "Black Muslim" must have been at the very least a slightly daunting proposition for many of Ali's opponents, especially the ones he christened "Uncle Toms".'

But in 1975 Ali had other matters than religion to consider.

Don King was promoting a third match between Ali and Frazier, and the President of the Philippines, Ferdinand Marcos, was anxious that the bout be staged in the capital of his country, Manilla. The fight was billed as 'The Thrilla in Manilla.'

There were clearly political reasons for Marcos hosting the fight. Marcos had declared martial law over the whole of the country in 1972. He used a Communist and Islamic insurgency as the pretext for severely limiting civil liberties and ruling by decree.

He hoped a fight between the two boxing greats would distract his people and postpone a growing revolution long enough for him to consolidate his power.

The United States government supported the anti-Communist President and were also happy for the fight to proceed.

It is not known is Ali was aware of the politics, and, if he was, what he thought of Marcos fighting Muslims and denying his people the liberties he himself was advocating for black Americans.

It is known however that he attacked his opponent, Joe Frazier, with the venom that had become so familiar to his hearers.

He called Frazier a 'gorilla.' He punched a gorilla doll, chanting 'It will be a killa and a thrilla and a chilla when I get the Gorilla in Manila.'

'Joe Frazier is so ugly,' he said. 'His mother told me that, when Joe was a little boy, every time he cried, the tears would stop, turn around, and go down the back of his head.'

'I don't want to knock him out. I want to hurt him.'

Ali later explained his behavior by saying that he wanted to make Frazier so blind with rage that he would be off his fight.

Even so, his barbs seemed to go beyond strategy. There is something very nasty about them even today.

Ali's preparations were interrupted by the sudden appearance of his wife Khalilah.

In the United States she had watched on TV, as millions of people around the world, Ali introduce his mistress to Marcos as his wife.

She confronted Ali, arguing vociferously with him in his hotel suite.

The fight was hard. Frazier seemed to have steadied himself against Ali's insults, which continued during the match.

At one point it became clear that Ali's technique of resting against the ropes and forcing his opponent to expend energy uselessly was working to Frazier's advantage. He could get in close to Ali and pick up momentum.

Shortly after the bell sounded for the sixth round Frazier delivered a left hook which knocked Ali against the ropes.

He recovered, but soon took another left hook in the head.

In the ninth round Ali told his trainer 'Man, this is the closest I've ever been to dying!'

A dazed Ali said 'They told me Joe Frazier was washed up.' 'They lied', Frazier retorted.

Ali continued in defensive mode until round 12. By then Frazier, face swollen and nearly blind in one eye could barely see the swings of his opponent.

Ali went in, targeting the swollen eye.

The sports writer Frank McGhee, writing for the *Daily Mirror*, described what happened in the thirteenth round.

'The main turning point of the fight came very late. It came midway through the thirteenth round when one of two tremendous right-hand smashes sent the gum shield sailing out of Frazier's mouth. The sight of this man actually moving backward seemed to inspire Ali. I swear he hit Frazier with thirty tremendous punches — each one as hard as those which knocked out George Foreman in Zaire — during the fourteenth round. He was dredging up all his own last reserves of power to make sure there wouldn't have to be a fifteenth round.'

Frazier's trainer, Eddie Futch, ended the fight in round 15.

Frazier protested but Futch said 'No one will forget what you did here today.'

What Frazier and his team didn't know was that Ali was about to quit, but his trainer Angelo Dundee would not allow it.

'Frazier quit just before I did,' he would tell his biographer, Thomas Hauser. 'I didn't think I could fight any more.'

After the fight Ali contacted Frazier son to apologize for his savage behavior toward him. The son responded that Ali should be apologizing directly to Frazier.

Although Ali expressed his remorse several times later in life he seems never to have done so directly.

Nevertheless, Frazier said he forgave Ali, in the year of his death, 2011.

After Manilla Ali's performance in the ring deteriorated.

On June 1 1976, after watching the wrestler Gorilla Monsoon (1937 – 1999) in a match held in Philadelphia, Ali removed his shirt and challenged Monsoon.

Monsoon lifted Ali, spun him, and dumped him. Ali was persuaded to walk away. It is not known if the confrontation was staged or not. It seems unlikely that after Manila Ali could be persuaded to throw a fight against anyone.

An exhibition bout in Tokyo against wrestler Antonio Inoki was certainly a publicity event.

Even so, Inoki's kicks caused blood clots and infection to Ali's legs and the match was declared a drawer.

On September 28 1976 Ali took on Ken Norton for the third time, at Yankee Stadium. Ali defended his title. He won on scorecards and the scores were close. He had taken a beating from Norton and it showed.

After the fight he announced his retirement from boxing. He would devote himself to religion.

But his retirement was short-lived. Ali won his next two fights, but his doctor Ferdie Pacheo tried to persuade him to quit.

Ali's kidneys were deteriorated from years of punishment. Ali and his team rebuffed Pacheo, and he resigned.

In February 1978 Ali lost his title to Leon Spinks, a fighter who had only seven professional fights to his name. He won it back, making him the only boxer to have gained the title three times, but the fight was hard and uninspiring.

Ali announced his retirement for the second time. Many would have seen this as a sensible decision. 'The Greatest' would retire with a new record before his waning powers became too obvious.

But Ali returned to fight Larry Holmes (b. 1949) for the World Boxing Council Heavyweight title.

The fight was not motivated by the desire for the glory, but rather the need for money.

The fight took place on October 2 1980. Holmes easily won.

He not only beat Ali but pounded him. The actor Sylvester Stallone watched the fight and said that the experience was like seeing an autopsy performed on a living man.

The audience was looking at the shell of Muhammad Ali. Ali could not respond. He could not swing. He just took the beating.

He was heard to scream with pain, something which fans had never heard before.

An anxious Angelo Dundee stopped the fight at the eleventh round.

What the onlookers did not know was that Ali's hands were starting to tremble and he was starting to stutter. This was the beginning of Parkinson's Disease, thought it would be diagnosed as such until 1984.

Holmes had been merciful. Seeing Ali in the state that he was, exhausted and unable to respond, he held back from delivering the beating he could have.

The Holmes fight was the only fight that Ali lost by knockout.

It was hoped that the Holmes fight would also be his last.

It was not to be. Incredibly, Ali fought one last time. On December 11 1981 Ali fought Trevor Berbick (1954 – 2006) in Nassau in the Bahamas.

Berbick had taken the title from Larry Holmes, and Ali wanted it for the fourth time.

There were grave concerns about Ali's health and deteriorating skills, so much so that no state athletic commission would grant him a boxing license until South Carolina did only four months before the scheduled fight.

Ali blustered about beating Berbick easily, but there was none of the old spirit in his voice.

The fight was promoted by James Cornelius, a member of the Nation of Islam, but Don King claimed that Berbick had given him option on his next three fights.

King flew to the Bahamas and attempted to have an injunction placed on the fight. He claimed he was attacked by Cornelius and his men there. Cornelius denied this, though a member of Ali's entourage, Jeremiah Shabazz, later confirmed King's story.

Many involved in the preparation and promotion, including Eddie Futch, agreed it was one of the most poorly staged fights they had been involved in.

'They did everything wrong all the way through,' said Futch.

Indeed, the promotion seemed on the point of collapsing, which prompted ticket prices to fall from $50 to $5. Furthermore, Berbick was threatening to withdraw from the fight over money.

The fight itself was unspectacular. Berbick was not considered an exceptional fighter. He seemed to be sparing Ali simply for the sake of keeping the fight going.

But in the last three rounds Berbick took total control of the ring without Ali delivering a single blow.

The fight was decided unanimously for Berbick.

Afterwards Ali said 'I think I'm too old. I was slow. I was weak. Nothing but Father Time. The things I wanted to do, I couldn't do. I was doing my best. I did good for a 39-year-old. I think I'm finished. I know it's the end. I'm not crazy. After Holmes, I had excuses. I was too light. Didn't breathe right. No excuses this time. I'm happy. I'm still pretty. I could have a black eye. Broken teeth. Split lips. I think I came out all right for an old man.'

Politics And Religion

Ali's supporters must have breathed a collective sigh of relief when Ali finally realized that he could no longer fight. He had pushed himself to the absolute limits. He had proven to himself that he had done the best that he could do.

Ali's speech had slowed and he occasionally slurred his words. Physicians ascribed this to brain damage caused by boxing.

But Ali had ignored this advice, instead choosing to rely on a New York University report that attributed his slurring to a 'psychosocial response.' This allowed him to fight Berbick.

Ali did not retire from public life. He seems to have developed a renewed interest in the world after his reappraisal of the Nation of Islam.

In 1974 he had visited a Palestinian refugee camp and encouraged the people in their struggle 'to liberate their homeland.'

In 1978 he participated in the Longest Walk, an event that brought attention to the status of Native Americans.

Besides social issues he was also interested in politics. The United States Government certainly regarded him as a potential political asset.

In 1979 the Soviet Union invaded Afghanistan. The US Government boycotted the upcoming 1980 Olympics Games in Moscow in protest and attempted to persuade other nations to join them.

President Jimmy Carter convinced Muhammad Ali to go on a tour of five African nations to persuade them to join the boycott.

Ali was well known and popular in Africa. The Rumble in the Jungle in 1974 left a legacy that remains strong to this day. Furthermore, Ali was genuinely anti-Communist.

The five targeted nations were Kenya, Tanzania, Liberia, Nigeria and Senegal.

Much as Ali was respected in these countries, he was no diplomat, and seems to have been badly prepared for the mission.

He was unaware that the Soviet Union was actually supporting liberation movements in those countries.

Further, the United States was supporting South Africa and its apartheid regime and ignoring calls for trade sanctions from the rest of Africa.

African countries also recalled how the United States had refused to support a boycott against New Zealand in the 1976 Olympics on account of its rugby team violating a UN sporting embargo against South Africa.

Nevertheless Kenya refused to participate in the 1980 Games.

In 1980 Ali campaigned for Democrat Jimmy Carter for the Presidency of the United States.

On June 4 1982 Ali and wife Veronica Porche met with Pope John Paul II in the Vatican.

The two heavyweights, each in their own sphere, exchanged autographs.

Despite their obvious differences they shared much in common. Both supported civil rights. Both were anti-Communist. Both saw religion as an influence that could be for good.

Both had enjoyed athletics, though they followed different careers.

But they shared more than either knew at the time. Ali would learn he had Parkinson's Disease in 1984. The Pope would be diagnosed in 2001. Both struggled with the debilitating affliction.

In 1984, the same year he was diagnosed with Parkinson's he publicly endorsed

Ronald Reagan for re-election to the Presidency of the United States.

Reagan's stance on civil rights issues was ambiguous at best. He had opposed the Civil Rights Act and the Voting Rights Act in 1965.

In 1980 Reagan said that the Voting Rights Act was 'humiliating the South.' He professed the President of the Confederation, Jefferson Davis, to be one of his heroes.

In 1988 he vetoed the Civil Rights Restoration Act, which made observation of civil rights a condition of receiving federal funding. Congress overrode the veto.

Reagan was also opposed to the institution of the Martin Luther King national holiday.

Ali's support of Reagan, especially after campaigning for a Democrat seemed strange.

Puzzled reporters asked Ali why he was endorsing a man who was on the record as opposing civil rights legislation.

Ali replied 'He's keepin' God in schools and that's enough.'

In 1988 Ali rode on a float at the Tournament of Roses Parade in Pasadena, California. The Parade is part of New Year's Day celebrations, but in 1988 the event was particular significant. 1988 was the bicentenary of the United States of America.

The sight of Ali in that parade was certainly a far cry from the youth who raged against the establishment and refused to acknowledge its legitimacy.

In 1990 Ali traveled to Iraq to meet Saddam Hussein to negotiate, successfully, the release of 15 American hostages. This was just before the 1991 Gulf War.

The endeavor was criticized by the White House and by much of the Press.

Surely the strangest hostage-release campaign of recent days has been the 'goodwill' tour of Muhammad Ali, the former heavyweight boxing champion,' the *New York Times* wrote . . . he has attended meeting after meeting in Baghdad despite his frequent inability to speak clearly'

Saddam secured a promise from Ali that he would bring 'an honest account' of the Iraq situation to the United States government.

He suffered much from Parkinson's during the visit to Iraq. Indeed, it almost jeopardized the mission. He ran out of medication but managed to secure some for the personal encounter with Saddam.

Ali's disease was making such activity more and more difficult. But he was determined that it should not defeat him.

In 2002 he went to Afghanistan as a UN Messenger of Peace. He promoted UN humanitarian efforts there, following the expulsion of the Taliban from Kabul in December 2001.

On July 12 2012 Ali held the Olympic Flag at the Opening Ceremony of the Summer London Olympics. He was helped by his wife Lonnie Williams, whom he married in 1986.

In retirement Ali spent much of his time in philanthropic endeavors.

He raised funds for the Muhammad Ali Parkinson Center in Phoenix, Arizona. He also supported the Make-A-Wish Foundation and the Special Olympics.

He opened the Muhammad Ali Center in his hometown of Louisville Kentucky.

'Many fans wanted to build a museum to acknowledge my achievements,' Ali said of the Center. 'I wanted more than a building to house my memorabilia. I wanted a place that would inspire people to be the best that they could be at whatever they chose to do, and to encourage them to be respectful of one another.'

In 2005 President George W. Bush awarded Ali the Presidential Medal of Freedom, the highest honor that can be awarded to a US citizen.

Ali's interest in religion was deepening at this time. He was drawn to the mystical side of Islam and Sufism in particular.

Followers of Sufism, in addition to following the precepts of Islam, including ritual prayer and fasting during Ramadan, engage in the mystical contemplation of God and meditation.

Sufism is probably most recognizable to outsiders through the spectacle of the whirling dervish.

These Sufi perform a dance aim to reach a state of union with Allah that empties the ego and surrenders the soul utterly to his love.

According to Yana Hasmeen, Ali's daughter by Veronica Porsche, his religious views have changed a lot since the heady days of militant black Islamism.

'My father is very spiritual-more spiritual now than he is religious,' she says. 'It was important for him to be very religious and take the stands he did in earlier years. It was a different time. He still tries to convert people to Islam, but it's not the same. His health and his spirituality have changed, and it's not so much about being religious, but about going out and making people happy, doing charity, and supporting people and causes'.

In December 2014 Ali was hospitalized for pneumonia. He recovered.

On January 15 2015 he was hospitalized again, this time on account of a urinary tract infection. He made a quick recovery and was discharged the following day.

But the end was near.

In Scottsdale, Arizona on June 2 2016 Ali was admitted to hospital with respiratory problems. His condition rapidly deteriorated, and by the following day he was suffering from septic shock. His vital organs were shutting down.

Ali was pronounced dead at 9.10 pm on June 4.

He was 74.

His daughter Hana tweeted the next day 'All of us were around him hugging and kissing him and holding his hands, chanting the

Islamic prayer… All of his organs failed but his HEART wouldn't stop beating. For 30 minutes...his heart just keep beating. No one had ever seen anything like it. A true testament to the strength of his Spirit and Will!'

Man And Icon

What should we make of the man who called himself 'The Greatest'?

There is a tendency for death to elevate an individual's achievements and to absolve that person from their sins. This is no doubt true of Ali as of any other deceased celebrity.

It is therefore difficult to assess the power and influence of a man who has died recently.

Undoubtedly he did much to further the cause of civil rights not only in his own country but throughout the world. Yet this cannot blind us to the fact that he did much to divide the world, especially during his angry Nation of Islam days when he was opposed to integration.

Undoubtedly many have been inspired by Ali to pursue their dreams. But it is fair to observe that Ali's ambition was highly aggressive. He was prepared to inflict not only physical injury upon his opponents but psychological violence as well. Though Joe

Frazier finally forgave Ali it is doubtful that he will ever forget what he did.

He was self-aggrandizing. He was brash. He was angry.

We might also comment on his relationships with women, particularly his second wife Khalilah, but perhaps this would be unfair.

It would however be fair to say that age, and illness, mellowed him, and encouraged him to seek peace with God, the world, and himself.

Certainly Ali's spirituality was a constant throughout his life, and his devotion to Islam and, in later years, the Sufi expression of that religion was undoubtedly genuine.

It has also been observed that Muhammad Ali the cultural icon serves to absolve us from seriously dealing with civil rights issues.

It has been sagely remarked that the canonization of Ali becomes a substitute for actually addressing the problems he spoke of. It is much easier, and cheaper, to build a statue and worship it, than to fight for racial equality.

After all, we did the same to Martin Luther King.

Ali called himself 'The Greatest.' How do we define greatness?

Perhaps greatness is not measured by a man's capacity to live up to their public image. All heroes ultimately fail, destroyed by the impossibility of their public image.

In his last years he certainly appeared to be a man who had let go of his image and embraced who he was.

Maybe greatness is rather the measure of an individual's ability to live who they truly are.

Writing for CBNC the journalist Jeff Cox kindly wrote on the subject 'In his later years, the indelible images of him were not the glory days in the ring, but of a shaking former boxer carrying the Olympic torch in 1996, or traveling around the world promoting humanitarian causes, and as an ambassador for humanity.

So when assessing Ali's "Greatest" claim, it is actually more productive to examine those later years, after his ring glory had ebbed and with his body wracked by an unrelenting foe. For all the conflict he stirred up in the national psyche during his younger years, his acts of charity, inspiration and his very public battle against Parkinson's erased all that.

The assessment, then, is complicated. Was Ali "the greatest" in the ring? It hardly matters at this point. His final lesson to the world was that greatness comes not just in the world of sport, but rather in life.'

If being great involves being the best, we can be and no more than greatness is surely within the grasp of everyone.

In His Own Words

The following are some excerpts from speeches made by Mohammad Ali.

1) From a reply to a question asked by a young English fan in 1977. He was asked what he would do when he retired.

'So what I'm gonna do when I get out of boxing? Is to get myself ready to meet God. Don't people die every day? It's a scary thing to think that I'm going to hell to burn eternally forever so what am I gonna do? When I get out of boxing or when I'm through I'm gonna do all I can to help people.

"He wants to know how do we treat each other, how do we help each other. So I'm going to dedicate my life to using my name and popularity to helping charities, helping people, uniting people. We need somebody in the world to help us all make peace. So when I die, if there's a heaven, I want to see it.

The most important thing is what's gonna happen when you die, are you going to go to heaven or hell, and that's eternity. How long is eternity? So what am I gonna do when I'm through fighting? I only have 16 years to be productive, get myself ready to meet God and go to the best place, does that make sense?'

2) From Ali's 1966 anti-war speech:

'Why should they ask me to put on a uniform and go 10,000 miles from home and drop bombs and bullets on brown people in Vietnam, while so-called Negro people in Louisville are treated like dogs and denied simple human rights? No, I am not going 10,000 miles from home to help murder and burn another poor nation simply to continue the domination of white slave masters of the darker people the world over. This is the day when such evils must come to an end. I have been warned that to take such a stand would put my prestige in jeopardy and could cause me to lose millions of dollars which should accrue to me as the champion.

But I have said it once, and I will say it again: The real enemy of my people is right here. I will not disgrace my religion, my people or myself by becoming a tool to enslave those who are fighting for their own justice, freedom and equality. If I thought the war was going to bring freedom and equality to 22 million of my people, they wouldn't have to draft me, I'd join tomorrow. But I either have to obey the laws of the land or the laws of Allah. I have nothing to lose by standing up for my beliefs. So I'll go to jail. We've been in jail for 400 years.'

3) Before the 1974 fight with George Foreman:

'Float like a butterfly, sting like a bee. His hands can't hit what his eyes can't see. Now you see me, now you don't. George thinks he will, but I know he won't.'

4) On life:

'Life is a gamble. You can get hurt, but people die in plane crashes, lose their arms and legs in car accidents; people die every day. Same with fighters: some die, some get hurt, some go on. You just don't let yourself believe it will happen to you.'

5) On terrorism:

'Terrorists are not following Islam. Killing people and blowing up people and dropping bombs in places and all this is not the way to spread the word of Islam. So people realize now that all Muslims are not terrorists'.

Made in the USA
Middletown, DE
15 January 2020